Dec. 2017

To Dorothy,

with all

best wishes.

In Christ's light,

Anne

Coudreaux

CHRIST IN THE DIGITAL AGE

Anne Coudreaux

ISBN-13: 978-1519613783
ISBN-10: 1519613784

Cover Design
Donna Overall

Book Design & Formatting
Donna Overall
donnaoverall@bellsouth.net

Independently published by
Anne Coudreaux
acoudreaux@gmail.com

৵

To D. and B., with love

Introduction

The following is a true story and, I hope, not too abstract.[1] Beginning in France, surfing over to the Pacific islands, then to the U.S. mainland, it tells of an unexpected journey of the spirit. I start with a wild and wondrous event, and then follow the journey in chronological order. No buzzwords are involved, such as quantum theory or mind vs. brain, because none is needed. The journey speaks for itself.

I wish to witness the creativity, freedom and love which are our birthright and of which Christ, with His revolutionary message, reminded us two thousand years ago—a message that still sings for our time.

1. Twelve squared

Launch out on [the] story, Muse…
Start from where you will — sing
for our time, too.
—Homer, The Odyssey[2]

On Sunday, December 2, 2012, I went to church, remembering my mother who had passed away eight years earlier, on the second day of December 2004. Having received the eucharist from Fr. George, I was walking in the nave when I became conscious of the presence of Christ, straightforward and unmistakable. Then I felt like my body was climbing two or three steps. And then… I was in the presence of God's love. A boundless universe of many dimensions, all of which were, and are,

1

love. And a surprising familiarity as well, in which I felt comfortable. This was the energy of Abba, our Father.

I walked back to my pew with the living presence of love in my heart and the simultaneous certainty I had been in a space beyond the universe as we know it through our senses, or our mind, our scientific knowledge and assumptions, our myths, our culture. This was an encounter beyond the uncertainty/indeterminacy principle, in full consciousness, "online" as neuroscientists say. I am not the first person to receive such a winged gift of grace. Here I wish to share it for our time, our digital age of information and communication. Bear with me: I am not a theologian or a mystic, only a geographer thirsty for knowledge.

That Sunday, 12/02/12, I came to call *Twelve squared:* a simple number to express a reality beyond numbers.

2. Way before the digital age

In the 1960s, when I was on vacation at my grandparents' home in the Loire Valley of France, I would practice my tennis game right in the street, hitting a ball against the big wall next to their house. There was no tennis court in the village; no one there played tennis. The cemetery was on the other side of the wall. A few steps away lay the workshop of my great-grandfather, a blacksmith, with its bellows and now silent anvil.

Occasionally a horse-drawn carriage would appear at one end of the street, giving me ample time to retrieve the ball. That ball would sometimes land in the cemetery, but no one complained.

Beyond the road to the nearest town, there was Paris, two hundred miles away. What lay beyond Paris, I wondered? What could the people there teach me?

My parents had lived through World War II and never talked about it to my brother and me. There were other things they never discussed with us, including religion, faith, or even skepticism about faith. In the heavily Catholic culture of post-war France, I was not raised a Catholic. Unlike most of my classmates, I did not attend catechism or go through the First Communion rite of passage. I did attend mass with my religious grandparents when I was on vacation with them in the summer.

And I liked reading Charles Péguy, who had returned to the faith of his youth and saw the cathedral in Chartres as a beacon of French values. Thanks to Péguy, I kept the possibility of faith open in my mind.

The spire of the cathedral was visible from far away over the flat plain of Beauce when we drove from Paris to my grandparents' home, yet my family never stopped in Chartres.

After college, I studied for an MBA in finance, worked in Paris for several years, traveled, moved to Hawaii to get a PhD in geography, married, and became a mother. I had roamed the earth to learn as much as I could, fulfilling the wish of my younger self. That was not enough, although I did not know it at the time. My spiritual life was still hidden from me.

3. First call

A great vision and small actions are what we need.

— Fr. J. Lemaire[3]

In the fall of 1988, wishing to expand my inner life, I signed up for a course in meditation and healing, which was taught in part by my husband, a transcultural and transpersonal psychiatrist. At the time, I believed in God, yet in a totally abstract way. I did not think He was interested in me. In brief, I was an outsider, in that area as most others in my life. Nothing new there.

I had admired the French nuns and two Catholic priests we had met in Papua New Guinea (PNG) in the late 1970s. Although

7

they understood I was not Catholic they did not proselytize. Their wish to serve others was evident, however. Reaching the mission involved a week of walking from the nearest town, Port Moresby, or flying in a small plane to the tiniest of landing strips on the side of a hill. The mission church was built out of branches and rough-hewn pieces of wood. On the Sunday we were there, there was a market. A lady offered me one grapefruit—the only item she had for sale.

The day before I was to attend the initial session of the course, I was going up the stairs to our apartment on the second floor. I looked down to the first floor landing, where my neighbor, Catherine, had just arrived from the parking garage in the basement. What I saw then startled me. Above the head of my neighbor there was an image of Christ several feet high. Christ was looking at me. A vivid sight, much larger and taller than an icon, which lasted a few seconds. My neighbor was Roman Catholic. I never told her about this experience.

The visual message was clear: Christ had opened the door and was now my neighbor in the inner space of soul.

4. Gift of the light

1989: the fall of the Berlin Wall, the bi-centennial of the French Revolution, the creation of the World Wide Web, the Slow Food Manifesto, a vivid year for change.

The course on meditation and healing was meeting once a month. In June 1989, during a practice session with a colleague, a sudden image pushed itself into my awareness. My eyes were closed, yet I could see the figure of a woman, dressed in a shimmering blue dress, her head covered with a veil. She moved closer. Her face was a constellation of pulsating light; her eyes were pure, transparent. My entire body began to feel the energy radiating from her. An intense energy of exploding love: each cell in my entire body could feel it. There was a lighted white candle in her hand, which she offered to me. I raised my arm very slowly, fighting the gravity of this physical world, to get hold of the candle. Once this was done, the lady in blue quickly receded into the distance and vanished. Her dress had a band of green at the bottom.

> *As a Light-bearing Candle, shining upon those in darkness we behold the Holy Virgin; for enkindling the celestial Light, She guides everyone to Divine knowledge; and by Her radiance illuminating the mind, may She be honored loudly as follows:*
> *[…]*
> *Rejoice! O Lightning illuminating the souls. […]*[4]

At the time I had not heard of the "Akathist Hymn," which sings the praises of the Holy Virgin and which is recited in part in Eastern Orthodox churches during the first four Fridays of Great Lent and in its entirety on the fifth Friday. There are 144 phrases in the Hymn, each one beginning with "Rejoice!"

In June 1989 Mary illuminated my soul, for which I am eternally grateful.

5. After 1989

Mary and Christ had opened the doors to my spiritual life. I started to explore it with the tools that were at my disposal. I was led by the search for learning, as the curiosity of my younger years had not left me. At the time religious syncretism was prevalent, and since my husband was professionally and personally involved in it, that is the first path I took. Simultaneously I started reading about spirituality, starting from the academic edge, as if I needed an intellectual hand to guide me. So Karen Armstrong's *A History of God* and historical accounts of the Christian faith and the Gospels were among the first books I read.

From my husband I learned about meditation in the Hindu and Christian traditions.

We visited the Christian mystic Stylianos Atteshlis (also known as Daskalos) in Cyprus. He had many followers at the time, mostly from Germany and Eastern Europe, who would listen to his lectures with rapt attention. Stylianos Atteshlis did not call himself a healer, saying that Christ is the healer. In his own way, he represented a bridge between psychotherapy and spirituality.

We traveled to New Hampshire to listen to an Indian guru and learn a mantra.

One day, a fellow who did call himself a healer had a meeting. He would look at a person in silence, and then the person would start crying and be healed. These were the days when healing was the catchword for all kinds of theories, books, and therapies. The search for healing was on. So the fellow looked at me for about three minutes and I was unable to shed tears (or laugh, for that matter). He said he would go into the kitchen and by the time he returned to the room hopefully I would be crying, because, he added, I was being really difficult and he had never met someone like me. When he returned I did start crying. A human reaction—I had been judged and found wanting. It was a power game: when he asked for compensation for his assistance, I refused to give it to him.

These inner experiences were new to me, enlarging my understanding. I only recount a few here. But an interior life, even a skilled interior life, is not necessarily a spiritual life. There was no inner encounter with most of those teachers, so-called healers, and the like. No spark, no joy, not even a certain amount of peace.

And then, one summer when I was in the French countryside with my parents, my mother told me I had been baptized in the Catholic Church when I was three months old. "What good did it do you?" she added. Plenty, it turned out.

6. The path of the heart begins

Quite a paradox: Christ had appeared to me when I was an adult, several years before I was told I had been baptized as an infant. I had been walking with Christ without knowing it. Now that I knew, my spiritual path became clearer.

In parallel with this new turn in my inner life, my outer life became a dissonant challenge that lasted ten years: divorce, illness in the family, rejection, humiliation, poverty, near homelessness, unemployment, layoffs, the life of a single mother, of an immigrant with then-useless diplomas and hardly any support system. By then I was no longer living in Hawaii but on the mainland. Storm-tossed, then surfing on roaring breakers, I survived. A friend lent me some money and I found work, always living on the edge.

Walking along the river near my home helped my body, mind and soul, *à la Thoreau*. During that time, I worked on a manuscript about nature as a source of insights and resilience.

I also attended the Greek Orthodox Church, often with my former mother-in-law and other family members, and started going to classes to learn about the faith. There was much to learn. Some people think they have been brainwashed as children, learning about the religion of their forebears, which gives them the incentive to leave religion behind as adults. I was not bound by such an idea and, therefore, embraced the teachings, which added communal weight to my personal experience.

To my surprise, the Chartres labyrinth had been rediscovered by Lauren Artress, a Canon of the San Francisco Episcopal Church. With my family, we had been driving by Chartres Cathedral every summer but did not know about the labyrinth. As a matter of fact, few in France knew about it… The Episcopal cathedral in my town installed an indoor canvas labyrinth through which anyone could walk on Friday afternoons. One day in 2000, I went there. As I walked slowly back from the center of the labyrinth, I felt God's peace and love in my heart. It was a physical presence, which was so deep, so embracing, that I could hardly walk for a few minutes after leaving the labyrinth and had to sit down. The Gospels offer words of encouragement; this gift was a different kind of encouragement, a sign of grace inscribed on my heart. Indeed St. Paul has stated that the new Covenant is written on "tablets… of the heart." *(2Co 3, 3)*

On September 10, 2001 a strange dream came to me during the night: first a street full of people, with tall skyscrapers in the background; then a cemetery with a giant slab of concrete, a huge grave, in the foreground. The next morning I was at home; a friend called and told me to turn on the TV. This is the only time I have had a precognitive vision.

7. Stepping into another world

A friend invited me to see an exhibit of Tibetan Buddhist art at a university gallery. A learned professor gave lectures on the topic. In a short while, I became enmeshed in the life of this man, whom I will call "X." I fell in love with him, or thought I had fallen in love. Naïveté and intellectual curiosity led me to an unknown territory, far and wide. X invaded my mind. For him it was a reasonable thing to do since he was showing me his world and sharing it with me.

At first I was in awe, as I discovered that I was equipped with the ability to receive images in my mind's eye and to be aware of the energy of others. In fact, all human beings are able to do so. This was undoubtedly the most interesting discovery of the adventure: there exists a level of consciousness beyond daily awareness, which shamans and other trained persons can access and of which all human beings partake via dreams and visions.

X introduced me to his world, but soon I realized that this was not a relationship based on mutual love. I could receive visual images and pieces of information via mind and body, but I was not given the tools to communicate with him in return. Except one time, when I thought of him and immediately realized my energy was next to his. He promptly removed that nonlocal communication tool. The relationship between us became one of teacher to student. Meanwhile, there was no contact between us in the material world. Once I saw him on campus, about fifty yards from me, and called his name, but he ran away and disappeared.

I sent X a letter by email, asking him to let me go and explaining that I was following the path of Christ. To no avail. The master/ disciple relationship continued, first with this person, then with lamas who took over from him. This involuntary servitude lasted several years. La Boétie (1530-1563), friend of Montaigne, coined the term "voluntary servitude" in connection with the socio-political system of his era. In my case, I had not even signed up for the lifelong voluntary servitude of the esoteric side of Tibetan religion.

What did that involve? I considered the experience as a geographer or anthropologist would and therefore wrote field notes nearly every day for a decade. Those who are interested may consult these notes. Here I am only writing from memory.[5] After the tumultuous beginning of this experience, around 2002-2003, when I unwillingly received a crash course in esoteric Tibetan religion, the power of habit took over. As La Boétie wrote, "All things become natural to human beings when they get used to them." And yet, he added, "only the person who wishes for simple and unaltered things holds onto their human nature." [6]

To sum up, there was contact every day and every night, in the form of visual images (still or moving) that communicated information, often in the guise of metaphors. During this period of my life, I was unable to dream, and the individualized processing of information between outer and inner life, which manifests in dreams, did not occur. Apart from X, the lamas never figured out that I was a woman or that I followed the path of Christ. They could see that I was not interested in practicing their skills in joint meditation and communication, and they often commented on that. For example, one of them sent the image of a huge, old, dirty, and out-of-order fridge to depict who (or what) I was. Another indicated that I lacked testosterone (feel free to imagine how to represent this notion in visual terms). All having fun at my expense so as to teach me self-effacement, I fathomed.

Contact also came by means of energy check-ups in various parts of my body, at any time of day or night, always physically painful to some degree, in part because the timing was generally unexpected. There is a continuum between mind and body, and between others' energy fields and ours; I learned that lesson well. The lamas used their minds to send messages of their presence to my body's nervous system. One morning, I received an enormous push of energy from one of them through the backside and into my heart. My blood pressure and pulse rose. After feeling ill all day, I eventually had to go to the emergency room by ambulance. The hospital released me around midnight when I felt better. No medical diagnosis was made.

Communication occurred through the senses of smell (for instance, I had offered incense sticks to X, and he would forward their fragrance in the middle of the night), vision (via images), touch (via body check-ups and electric jolts), and hearing (various noises would come through, such as knocking on a door). Communication took place wherever I happened to be, in the United States or France; physical distance was not a deterrent.

X and his colleagues live in a space of shamanistic consciousness (for lack of a better word; indeed this type of Buddhism is grounded in ancient shamanistic practice)—a space which becomes conscious at a certain level of awareness. Love to them is a form of energy under the command of mind, not an end in itself, and it can be used as a Trojan horse, as I experienced it. I wrote several emails to X, asking him to stop these communications, to which he did not respond. The first and last communication that I received from him in the physical world was: "Please do not keep sending me emails or presents. I wish you well but please don't be under the illusion that there is a relationship between us." But in the meantime he did not stop sending messages on the other, alternate, level of consciousness.

Theirs is a closed society, a secret society. Once at an art lecture I happened to meet a lama and spoke, between the lines, of various ways to communicate. That night a painful electric shock between my legs was punishment for going beyond the lines.

It took years for me to disentangle body and mind from the secret society through prayer, patience, and contemplation. I never lost faith in God and kept the course, even as I felt stranded and lonely. Day after day, Saint Silouan's words guided me: "And the Lord answered my soul: *'Hold your mind in hell and do not despair.'"* [7]

After liturgy one Sunday in December 2014, love, peace and compassion came through and I realized that we are all trying very hard, including Tibetan Buddhists.

8. Return to Ithaca

The journey of the heart went on, whatever the outer and inner circumstances of my life. In 2004 my parents unexpectedly passed away within months of each other, my father in August and my mother on December 2. I moved temporarily to France to take care of certain matters following their passing.

In early January 2005, I was in Paris. It was very cold. After seeing a friend for coffee, I was walking in the street when I suddenly felt the energy of my mother. How can I explain it? I recognized her instantly in my heart. She was sending a message of love, indicating that everything was all right for her on the other side of physical death. I stopped on the sidewalk; our two hearts merged. Perhaps this contact lasted a few seconds, perhaps longer, but only the intensity mattered, not the time or place. Thank you, *Maman*, of blessed memory.

Again, life was not easy, with many issues of importance to deal with. The beautiful churches of Paris were my haven. I liked one in particular, on the Ile St. Louis, one of two small islands in the Seine River. The other, Ile de la Cité, is home to Notre-Dame Cathedral. I remember praying and opening my heart to God in that church one day when people were venerating the Holy Sacrament, symbolized by the light of a candle. When I walked out of the church a white-hatted chef and his cooking staff were enjoying the fresh air in front of a restaurant on the other side of the street. We spoke for a while, in full conviviality, even though I was not a customer. Down the street is a well-known ice-cream shop, where I stopped for a cone on the way.

In the spring of 2006, I was still living in France. In Notre-Dame Cathedral, the crown of thorns is shown to the public once a month. Louis IX (the future St. Louis), King of France, purchased it from the Eastern Latin Empire in Jerusalem. When the crown, said to be worn by Christ during His crucifixion, arrived near Paris in 1239, the king walked there barefoot to welcome it.

Wishing to pay homage to the crown, I took the subway from home, in a suburb west of Paris, and then walked — but not barefoot — to the cathedral where I was surprised to see many people, even though it was a weekday. The long line in the middle of the nave was moving slowly, as each person in turn would stand in front of the crown, which is encased in a transparent tube, and kiss it. As I waited, I called on all my family members to be present with me. I arrived in front of the crown, moved one step forward, and kissed it. As I walked back to my seat, Christ manifested His presence to me, beyond time and space, beyond the mind —a living presence of unconditional love. His presence, a lifting breeze, stayed with me for the entire day. I could distinguish both the divine and human nature of Christ. And in that human nature there was lightness and even humor!

Why this pure gift of grace? I will not try to explain it. I just wish to share it with others. In any case, it made me realize that Christ will look out for lost sheep, like me, who did not know for a long time that she had been baptized. Also, Christ let me experience who He is. He left it up to me, in full freedom, to know the difference between Eastern mysticism and His path. "Hello, here I am, no strings attached, only tenderness, call on me if you wish" — that was the message. It has been known by seekers for two thousand years and here I received it anew, fresh like the morning dew, totally personal, friendly, human and divine both.[8]

Back in the United States, I committed to the Greek Orthodox Church by being chrismated (sealed with the Holy Spirit) in 2007, which allowed me to take communion (eucharist) in thanksgiving. A slow path for this procrastinator, since Christ had appeared to me in 1988 and this was nineteen years later. Receiving the eucharist for the first time was a joyful event, mixed with awe.

Why the Greek Orthodox Church? I am not Greek, but I think the Eastern Orthodox Church is the closest to the path of Christ, as my mind, soul, and spirit have experienced it. And I had been attending church with my former husband's Greek American family for many years (without taking communion), so a feeling of kinship also played a part in my decision.

I have not turned my back on the Catholic Church, the Orthodox Church's close cousin. All the churches and chapels that dot Europe are magnificent witnesses to the faith of our forebears. Mont St. Michel in western France is an architectural and spiritual marvel, again surrounded by the sea and its great tides now that the road to it has been replaced by a bridge. As a matter of fact, the next episode in my spiritual life took place in a church in R., the French village where I have a house inherited from my parents. That Sunday in the fall of 2011, two neighbors and I were in church after doing the harvest in their vineyard the previous day. Grape harvesting by hand is disappearing, replaced by machines, because labor is hard to find. And yet *faire les vendanges* is good comradeship. Perhaps it should be marketed to corporations as a team-building exercise. So, there we were, my friends and I...

During mass something softly pushed my head to the right, in the direction of a statue of Jesus Christ whose hands were showing his heart. And then, as I looked at the statue, a whiff of love from it carried a message: I was a human being and as such I was worthy. Yes, worthy, *digne* in French. Worthy to love and be loved as a person. I had very much doubted that notion, given the circumstances of my life in the previous weeks and generally since I was a child. Personal details do not matter here. What matters is that this message is for all of us, because we have all been wounded, in one way or another. Another timely gift, received gratefully.

After my father passed away, I discovered an official document that indicated that during World War II, when he was in the underground French Resistance movement, he had once safeguarded the lives of fellow resisters under enemy fire. He and my mother had always been very discreet about their experience of the war, so this was a surprising discovery. Alas, my father died a violent physical and emotional death. But the visual and tactile message I received from him one night last year was in keeping with his life: he was accompanied by several kindred acolytes who showed me a story of joy and friendliness, a gift that uplifted soul and body, not with an electric jolt but with a touch of physical tenderness. And then they were gone, to their next adventure. (Perhaps, like them, we will spend our heaven in service to others, wherever they are...) This message was different from the one I had received from my mother in early 2005 yet reassured me. Thank you, dear father and friends. May your memory be eternal.

The intriguing part about my father's message was the fact that the story he and his colleagues shared that night indicated that they knew much about my life: the story involved an acquaintance of mine, whom my father had never seen or even heard of (she visited me in Paris after his passing). In other words, my life story is like a database, available and accessible at a level of consciousness beyond daily human consciousness. They had accessed this database and imagined a story from it. I appreciated their brilliantly conceived and unexpected gift, as short-lived as it was.

❧

Today, the most obvious sign of modernity in the place where I spent youthful summers is that horse-drawn carriages are long gone, replaced by tractors. My parents sold my grandparents' home years ago; we kept the bellows and some of the dusty horse collars that were in the blacksmithing workshop. A new tennis and basketball court stands on the southern edge of the village. Freshly baked bread from the bakery is available; so is internet access.

Who now wants to see the vast universe beyond the court, beyond the village, and beyond the World Wide Web? It still awaits our exploring.

Love—

Not attachment or non-attachment

Not desire or absence of desire

A blessing, a pathway, a personal choice

Made in freedom

Open to all—

The core of one's heart

The ground of beingness

Both human and spiritual.

Alive in the world but not of the world.

Love never ends.

Love never dies.

Love is.

—2006

9. Joy is peace dancing

Advance on your own path, for it only exists through your walking.
— St. Augustine (354-430)

Each one of us is unique; each one of us needs to advance on his or her own path. I can only share what I have learned experientially, after starting, when I was younger, from a tabula rasa in terms of faith and trust.

Here is the most evident and important to me, but perhaps the least reasonable in this day and age (a scandal for those in mind's hold?):

- God is, and so are Christ, the Holy Spirit, and Mary (*Theotokos* in Greek).

- There is life after death.

- God gives us what we need to progress spiritually.

- God is love.

- The true nature of Abba is revealed by Christ.

- Each human being is a son or a daughter of God.

Today there is a conflict between science and faith. Yet they are compatible. God does not ask us to let go of intelligence as we explore the physical universe and, now, the multi-layered space of consciousness. We are in His image. The only thing we have to work on is to be more in His resemblance, i.e., loving.

This reality is not an illusion. It is a training ground for building up creativity, freedom, interaction with others, and love in our lives. Christ showed us the way: no love without freedom to love, while creativity allows us to best express our love with one another in a unique way, depending on circumstances.

Creativity, freedom and love cannot be reduced to algorithms. Christ consciousness is beyond mathematical modeling, machine learning, and artificial intelligence. Human beings cannot be totally replaced by computers as long as they have a heart and put their mind into their heart.

Experimenters are now pushing the boundaries of reality into virtual reality and augmented reality. Without any "high-tech" gadgets, we can all participate in expanding the space of our heart. It is not an experiment but a calling based on goodwill, to fruitful effect.

Love is the highest level of consciousness. Therefore, by loving one another through giving and sharing (as well as solidarity, reconciliation, thoughtfulness, peace-building, justice…), we are already there. Initiation into a secret society or esoteric knowledge is not a prerequisite for the practice of love in action ("charity").

There is a circular economy of love, in which all participate: Abba, Christ, the Holy Spirit, and us, as long as we wish to belong. It is teamwork! Come as you are, with your own voice. One can also call this space of love an ecosystem, or an *oikoumene*. Geographers, who are place 'and space-oriented by definition, appreciate that Greek word, also spelled *ecumene*, which means "a place where we live and we can live." [9]

Love backward: forgive and let go of resentment. Love forward: share, give, without expectations, without measuring efficiency or efficacy. There is no spiritual accounting involved, it is not a "pay forward" philosophy with expectations of future positive karma. Love in action is both the goal and the reward. Let us improvise as we go along. Those love notes are played in the heart. "You can live by it," as the great trumpeter and singer Louis Armstrong said about jazz.

Fr. Seraphim: "Have a heart, and you will be saved. Every morning, see where your heart is and go where it leads you." [10]

Love begets peace, rather than the other way around. And love begets joy, as well. Joy is peace dancing... Advance on your own path, for it only exists through your dancing, to paraphrase St. Augustine...

Christ teaches us to welcome the other; when we welcome Him, we can welcome everyone we meet. Throughout our lives, we can feed a multitude with our loving words and actions, just as Christ once fed five thousand people. *"You give them something to eat,"* He told His disciples. *(Mark 6:37)*

≈

The living message of Christ fits in well with the digital age, which is characterized by the "three Cs": connection, community, and creativity.

Instant connection is vital in today's world. To communicate with the Trinity, and simply to be open to be touched by it, one can pray, contemplate, listen, and be grateful. I do so every day. Attending liturgy and especially receiving the eucharist are essential forms of connection. One can study the scriptural texts and the books that assuage one's spiritual curiosity. Recently I picked up Fabrice Hadjadj's "anti-manual of evangelization" because I like this author's sense of humor.

No one said spiritual literature should be dull.

The economy / ecosystem / *oikoumene* of love is all about community. All human beings are invited to participate and to enrich their lives through mutual interaction. That's even better than the internet, where one has to pay for access and needs tools. The *agape* community is free access, at all times and in all locales. Forever.

And, finally, creativity. One can be creative with one's personal "database" by letting go of what weighs one down. There are tools, notably through contemplative visualization, for releasing negative thoughts and feelings such as resentment. And creating for the general good is one way to be part of the economy of love. Here the digital age is ahead, with collaborative platforms such as online encyclopedias, open-source software, crowdfunding projects, and the like. The digital age, in selfless service, coalesces with "Christ in the digital age," the title of this essay.

Freeing that spirit of service and innovation makes the authentic message of Christ sing for our time.

And now, onward and online @ the *oikoumene* of love!

❧

Notes

(1) Sixty years ago the writer Albert Camus called for followers of Christ to "come out of abstraction" and speak their truth in the midst of the sound and fury of human history. Cf. Guillebaud, p. 9.

(2) Homer, p. 77, lines 11-12.

(3) Fr. Jean Lemaire, a priest in the village of R., in the Loire Valley: "Il faut de grandes visions et de petits gestes." (2014)

(4) The Akathist Hymn, p. 97.

(5) Under a pen name, Dionysios Farasiotis wrote about similar experiences of Eastern spirituality in a book originally published in Greek in 2001. I recommend the reading of this book, which has been translated in English, to anyone who wants to know about the temptation of spiritual power confronted to love as spiritual truth.

(6) «Si toutes choses deviennent naturelles à l'homme lorsqu'il s'y habitue, seul reste dans sa nature celui qui ne désire que les choses simples et non altérées.» *(Discours de la servitude volontaire,* my translation) La Boétie wrote the text in 1548. It was published for the first time in 1574.

(7) These words are from Silouan 1976/1994, p. 57 (my translation from the French). St. Silouan explains that he confronted demons brought about by his pride.

(8) Today the crown of thorns is located in a side chapel in the cathedral, inside an opaque plastic box, and therefore barely visible. It is shown to the public once a month and during Holy Week.

(9) Patriarch Bartholomew, "Building bridges: interfaith dialogue, ecological awareness, and culture of solidarity," Address to the Izmir University of Economics, February 9, 2015. Source: **www.OMHKSEA.org**, posted February 11, 2015.

(10) In Leloup, p. 97 (my translation from the French).

References

The Akathist Hymn. The original Greek text with a new translation by Father George Papadeas. South Daytona, FL: Patmos Press, 2002.

Artress, Lauren. *Walking a Sacred Path: Rediscovering the Labyrinth as a Spiritual Practice.* New York: Riverhead Books, 1995, 2006.

Farasiotis, Dionysios. *The Gurus, the Young Man, and Elder Paisios,* translated and adapted by Hieromonk Alexis (Trader). Platina, Calif.: St. Herman of Alaska Brotherhood, 2008.

Guillebaud, Jean-Claude. *Comment je suis redevenu chrétien.* Paris: Albin Michel, 2007.

Hadjadj, Fabrice. *Comment parler de Dieu aujourd'hui? Anti-manuel d'évangélisation.* Paris: Salvator, 2012.

Homer. *The Odyssey*. Translated by Robert
Fagles. New York: Penguin Group, 1996.

Leloup, Jean-Yves. *Lettres à un ami athée*. Paris:
Philippe Rey, 2008.

Silouan. *Ecrits spirituels, extraits*. Begrolles-en-
Mauges: Abbaye de Bellefontaine, 1976/1994.
Spiritualité orientale, no. 5.

+

Made in the USA
Charleston, SC
15 February 2017